Social Skills Training for Children

by
Martin Herbert

BPS BOOKS THE BRITISH PSYCHOLOGICAL SOCIETY

First published in 1996 by BPS Books (The British Psychological Society), St Andrews House, 48 Princess Road East, Leicester LE1 7DR, UK.

Transferred to digital print 2004

A catalogue record for this book is available from the British Library.

ISBN 1 85433 194 9

Typeset by Ralph Footring, Derby.

Printed in Great Britain by Athenaeum Press Ltd., Gateshead, Tyne & Wear

Contents

Social skills training for children

Introduction

Skill comes so slow, and life so fast doth fly,
We learn so little and forget so much.

(Sir John Davies, 1569–1626)

Aims

The aims of this guide are to provide the practitioner with:

1. a description of the nature of social skills;
2. an account of the main theories relating to social skills training;
3. a description of assessment and treatment issues;
4. some examples of a behavioural approach to social skills training.

Objectives

When you have read this guide you should be able to:

1. define inappropriate/dysfunctional social behaviour/skills;
2. put forward explanatory hypotheses for such difficulties;
3. conduct an assessment and negotiate intervention goals;
4. plan an intervention (social skills training/antisocial behaviour reduction);
5. provide parents with helpful hints in the form of handouts.

The nature of social skills

Apart from the obvious skills such as learning to read and write, crossing the road safely, counting the correct change, there are certain skills which, because they are not obvious or readily taught, come hard to some youngsters. These are the social skills that we use when we meet strangers, make small talk, encourage acquaintanceship, attract friends and fit in with groups of people.

From early childhood we have to learn how to react to, and cope with, a multitude of people and situations. Many conventions shape our behaviour towards particular persons in particular circumstances – there are some things that can be said and others that cannot. A familiarity of manner and address which is permissible with one individual, is frequently taboo with another; there are sensitivities, about both topics and language, which must be respected if offence is not to be given in certain settings and to certain people. We have to learn to predict and interpret the behaviour of others.

Childhood behaviour problems are, by and large, exaggerations, deficiencies, or handicapping combinations of behaviours common to *all* children. In childhood, the behaviour problems (unlike those of adults) are predominantly of the deficit kind. A minority (but a *substantial* minority) of children, for a variety of reasons which remain somewhat obscure, lack some of the crucial skills required to cope with life in a satisfactory manner. Consequently, they behave maladaptively in response to a variety of stresses, frustrations and challenges. Most children, for example, learn the social skills of mastering their temper and other anti-social behaviour; there is a lot to learn in becoming a member of society.

Coercive behaviours

From early on, children have a repertoire of some 14 **coercive behaviours**, including temper tantrums, crying, whining, yelling and commanding, which they use (wittingly or unwittingly) to influence their parents. At times, as most parents learn, influence develops into outright manipulation and confrontation. The older 'aggressive' boy or girl displays coercive behaviours at a level commensurate with a two- to three-year-old child and, in this sense, is an exemplar of arrested socialization. What usually happens is that with increasing age, certain coercive behaviours such as whining, crying and tantrums are no longer acceptable to parents; these behaviours then become the target for careful monitoring and sanctions, which in turn are accompanied by reductions in their frequency and intensity. Children also learn alternative, socially acceptable strategies for expressing their wishes and achieving their ends. Thus social skill is an important element in making aggressive behaviour redundant.

By the age of four, there are substantial improvements in a child's ability to hold in check their negative commands, destructiveness and attempts to coerce by aggressive means. By five, most children use less negativism, non-compliance, and negative physical acts.

Lack of friends

Repeated episodes of verbal and physical aggression lead to children being disliked, rejected and ridiculed by other children. Moreover, the parents of the non-aggressive children do not want their children to associate with the aggressive child. Consequently, these misbehaving children are rarely invited to birthday parties or to play after school with other children. If such youngsters can be helped to become more flexible and competent, then they may have less recourse to problem behaviour. A lot is at stake if they lack social skills.

Frequently parents report that their child has no friends. Feedback from teachers and other parents is an important indicator for parents that their children are not like other children. It is also a key element in the tension between parents of conduct-disordered children and parents of other normal children, contributing to their own feelings of rejection and isolation.

Non-compliance and defiance

Another dominant characteristic of children who are resisting social training as described by their parents, is their non-compliance accompanied by defiance. Parents report that their children's refusal to comply to parental requests controls not only the parents, but the entire family, by virtue of the power commanded through their resistance.

Benefits of social skills training

The behavioural techniques developed for Social Skills Training (SST) and other areas, appear to offer particular advantages for the helping professions in cases where traditional approaches have been found deficient. For example, they can be used with less able and non-verbal children and those displaying anti-social behaviour who may lack the behavioural repertoire necessary for achieving more appropriate behaviour.

Socially skilled children

Socially skilled individuals, it is postulated, are better able to deal with provocative situations by compromise, persuasion, relaxation, humour and other appropriate responses, which not only reduce the provocation but also preserve self-esteem without resort to extremes.

By contrast, persons who lack social skills have limited choices when it comes to dealing with aggravations and are likely to become aggressive, for example, more readily. Socially successful children have at their command more potential techniques for solving everyday person-to-person dilemmas. The processes involved here are sensitivity to when problems occur, the ability to imagine alternative courses of action and sensitivity to the consequences of an action.

Socially unskilled children

Socially unskilled children may display a variety of problems, ranging from social withdrawal, shyness, and isolation, to aggressive anti-social behaviour. Those who tend towards aggressive behaviour search for fewer clues as to the appropriate response and generate fewer appropriate solutions to conflict situations. They produce a higher percentage of aggressive and incompetent solutions than co-operative children do, and have a more difficult time anticipating the consequences of their solutions. They act aggressively and impulsively without stopping to think of non-aggressive solutions.

Academic performance, mental health and emotional well being, school adjustment, proneness to delinquency, peer relationships, and adult adjustment are some of the areas adversely affected by extreme and continuing deficits in social functioning. 'Success breeds success' may be a cliché, but it has a respectable empirical basis. For those children who fail to exhibit the requisite skills for gaining peer acceptance, failure does indeed breed failure. Take the vicious cycle of poor peer relationships; children with peer problems tend to become aggressive or antagonistic towards other children, or they withdraw from them – not surprisingly, they are rejected by their peer group. If children fail to develop social confidence they tend to feel generally inadequate; the more inadequate they feel, the more likely they are to fail.

What is 'skill'?

Skill is defined most commonly as the utilization of a complex set of behaviours in order to accomplish a task. It should be possible to break down any task into its component abilities, each of which is necessary for successful task performance. There is a clear analogy with problem-solving in a particular person-to-person setting. Does the child have a number of alternative courses of action (solutions) which s/he can take, plus some means of choosing between them; or are they tied to narrow, rigid and perhaps self-destructive modes of action – aggression being a classic example? When a practitioner sets out to help an unskilled child, the aim is to increase the child's repertoire of possible actions within an interpersonal setting, making his/her relationships with peers both more constructive and more creative.

Part I: Assessing social skills

Many children, as they grow up, are socially unskilled (after all they are learners in life); they may be shy, socially gauche, inappropriate – indeed, plain antisocial. So what is the point at which social insensitivity or fear, or, indeed, other behaviour, is thought to be counterproductive and thus dysfunctional? Our mental alarm bells would begin to ring if there was a marked quality of age-inappropriateness, extremeness (in terms of frequency and/or intensity) or persistence (duration) of the shyness, say, or antisocial behaviour. Large deficits in skills that were leading to social rejection or other handicapping would be worrying. Our concern would increase also if there were many other coexisting problems. This is illustrated in *Table 1*.

Table 1. Behaviour giving cause for concern

Behaviour	Frequency	(high rates of, say, anti-social, or insensitive behaviour)
	Intensity	(extreme, e.g. crippling social anxiety, persistent, intractable anti-social actions)
	Number	(several coexisting problems)
	Duration	(long enduring 'chronic' social difficulties)
	Sense/meaning	(bizarre, un-understandable socially inappropriate behaviours)

One aim of SST is to address these issues (see Herbert, 1986; 1987) within the context of a broadly conceived behavioural programme.

Another specific aim of SST is to make good deficits in interpersonal skills so that the child will gain peer acceptance. A fundamental problem in the assessment of social skills is the absence of agreement among would-be assessors on a clear definition of social competence. This means that there are no precise, generally accepted external criteria against which to validate and cross-validate the plethora of assessment methods.

Gresham (1981) performed factor analyses on measures obtained from different sources and concluded that *peer ratings*, *peer nominations*, and *direct observations* measure independent dimensions of social competence. The conditions in which social skills are evaluated rarely attempt to identify whether the children *actually* have deficits, that is, whether the requisite responses are in their repertoires but are just not being elicited (Kazdin, Esveldt-Dawson and Matson, 1981). Under standardized assessment conditions, no attempt is made to maximize performance to see if the skills are actually present. Kazdin *et al.* believe that changes within the conditions of assessment might lead to marked changes in the social skills children display. Kazdin *et al.* showed that positive reinforcement during social skills assessment could markedly influence performance. Since we are forced, at present, to use *subjective* criteria to define social adjustment, we need to obtain multiple measures from different social agents if we are to agree on a definition of social competence.

Goal setting and social competencies

Treatment goals in the area of social skills are based upon value judgements of what are socially appropriate behaviours. The literature suggests some specific notions about what makes a child socially successful or unsuccessful and I will now outline these.

(i)   Children who are highly acceptable to their peers tend also to show sensitivity, responsiveness and generosity in their interactions with their peers. They help others often, they give attention, approval and affection often to others, they give and receive friendly overtures and respond positively to the dependent behaviour of their peers, and they are sensitive to the social overtures of other children.

(ii) Children who are not much liked by others, but also not particularly disliked, tend to be withdrawn, passive, and fearful of social contact.

(iii) Children who are actively disliked by others tend to be aggressive. They seem to get locked in a cycle whereby they learn that to get what they want they should be aggressive; this often succeeds in the short-term (for example, they get a toy by using threats) but fails in the long-term in that other children avoid and reject them. In this way, the aggressive children never learn alternatives to their actions, and become more and more reliant on aggression as their only social skill.

(iv)   Children who are well-liked are better at seeing things from the point of view of another child; disliked children tend to be poor at this.

(v)   The most effective, most socially competent individuals are particularly sensitive to *non-verbal* communications. Popular children are socially sensitive, as can be gauged from the rich, complex and highly-organized descriptions they give of other children.

(vi)   Many other things determine how successful a child will be in a social setting – for example, how attractive s/he is, how bright, good at sports, amusing (Herbert, 1974).

(vii)   There seem to be two basic attitudes which should be enhanced if a child is going to make friends with reasonable ease:

(a)   the perception of other people as sources of satisfaction rather than deprivation;

(b)   the child has opportunities for social interactions that reward and make enjoyable the giving, as well as the receiving, of affection.

Antecedents of social skills problems

The situational model

The assumption here is that some children fail to fully develop proficiency (or lose it) due to lack of opportunity to practise or use skills. It is crucial to analyse the situational factors in social deficit problems, such as difficulty in making friendships.

Some settings are better than others at engendering good social relations: thus, schools with a high turnover of children are bad places to learn interpersonal skills because of the instability of the peer group; classes organized on small-group, co-operative lines may be particularly good for encouraging the development of constructive interpersonal skills. But on top of this there is something about the use that a child makes of his/her personal qualities.

The social learning model

The assumption underlying the skill-deficit model is that the child's incompetencies are the result of faulty socialization or ineffectual learning. The most important foundations for learning social skills are probably the relationships which children form with adults and with other children. Through these relationships a child learns how to locate him/herself in a social world, form emotional bonds, and understand the complex social events with which s/he may be presented.

Parental attitudes

A careful analysis should be made of the types of social situation which upset the child. Parental attitudes such as over-solicitous concern about the child foster timidity, providing a cue for the child to behave in a dysfunctional manner when in the company of others. Parents thus become part of the intervention. It may be they themselves who, by excessively authoritarian discipline or excessively *laissez-faire* attitudes, produce negative self-attitudes in the child.

The interference model

The interpretation here is that specific skills are, in fact, present but not employed because emotional or cognitive factors interfere with their performance. The 'process' of working out appropriate goals and strategies of monitoring and setting standards and then adjusting and controlling one's actions may be faulty. This could result from severe anxiety, erroneous self-attributions and low self-esteem.

Bandura's (1977) self-efficacy theory attempts to explain the mutual interactional influences of people's self-perceptions and their behaviour. People who are low in perceived self-efficacy believe they cannot produce positive outcomes which leads to a sense of helplessness and an avoidance of feared situations and a vicious cycle of fear and performance-failure is established. There is no opportunity for a child caught in this cycle to develop new social skills, let alone practise old ones.

Immature, self-centred children are not always able to manage the give-and-take of friendship. Exchange theory gives us pointers to why this should be so; it provides one method of evaluating friendships and of helping children to improve their social attractiveness. A notable feature of friendship is the balance in the relationship that exists between the partners, often called 'status symmetry'. It concerns the mutual respect and lack of dominance and exploitation which characterize intimate and lasting relationships, involving an overall balance in the influence of each of the participants in friendly relationships. Benefits of the relationship outweigh 'costs'.

Part II: Intervention: social skills training

All the factors just described need to be considered in planning a social skills or antisocial behaviour-reduction programme.

The majority of studies evaluating the effectiveness of SST has been conducted on children with *behavioural problems* such as un-assertiveness, excessive aggression, and social withdrawal. The results – reducing antisocial behaviours and making good deficits in prosocial behaviour – are highly encouraging (see Combs and Slaby, 1977; Ladd, 1994; Herbert, 1993).

There have been few studies of developmentally *delayed or retarded* children, but those which have been conducted have been promising. Other work has focused specifically on skills training in school, and the findings, again, are generally positive. Helping unpopular, rejected children to improve the quality and quantity of relationships with peers has also been a matter of concern.

SST for children, as with other groups, is usually comprised of several treatment strategies: modelling, instruction, shaping, feed-back, behaviour rehearsal and reinforcement, sometimes combined. Exposure to socially inadequate models or insufficient exposure to socially skilled models, may leave the child unskilled in social interactions. According to principles of observational learning, new responses can be acquired and responses already in the child's repertoire can be facilitated, inhibited or disinhibited by imitation.

Much SST training is *content-orientated*, that is, the teaching of specific, complex skills. A cognitive approach tends to be more *process-orientated* (that is, problem-solving) although children's knowledge of social exchange norms and awareness of their own special impact upon others would be seen as crucial to their ability to 'read' social situations realistically and with sensitivity. We know that faulty attributions, negative beliefs and unrealistic expectations may lead to maladaptive behaviours (Herbert, 1986) in social interactions. Such matters would certainly be high among the concerns of the cognitively-orientated behaviour therapist. But s/he would be committed, too, to helping the child to 'unravel' knotty social situations, to analyse them and to generate alternative solutions to the self-defeating strategies so far adopted. Ladd (1994), adopting a cognitive-social learning model, views effective social functioning as being dependent upon the child's:

(i)   knowledge of specific interpersonal actions and how they fit into different kinds of person-to-person situation;

(ii)   ability to convert knowledge of social nuances into the skilled performance of social actions in various interactive contexts;

(iii)   the ability to evaluate skilful and unskilful behaviour accurately and to adjust their behaviour accordingly.

Behavioural methods

Modelling

The purpose of the application of modelling is to bring about change in a wide variety of behaviours. It can be used effectively in at least three situations:

1. acquiring new or alternative patterns of behaviour, from the model, which the client has never manifested before (for example, social skills, self-control);

2. the increase or decrease of responses already in the client's repertoire through the demonstration by high prestige models of appropriate behaviour (for example, the disinhibition of a shy, withdrawn client's social interactions), or the inhibition of learned fears – for example, avoidance of gym – or the suppression of impulsive antisocial behaviour which gets in the way of social relationships; and

3. the increase in behaviours which the observing client has already learned and for which there are no existing inhibitions or constraints.

Three variations of modelling – *filmed modelling, live modelling* and *participant modelling* – tend to be used.

Contingent reinforcement

Adult attention is a primary source of reinforcement for children. Social interactions can be beneficially or adversely affected by the reinforcement history experienced by the growing child. Bandura (1977) has listed a number of ways in which lack of learning or faulty social learning could occur.

1.   Insufficient reinforcement may lead to the extinction of appropriate behaviours. The child might receive little attention or no reward from unthinking, harsh or neglectful parents.

2.   The child may receive inappropriate reinforcement for what is generally considered undesirable behaviour. Reinforcement of socially prohibited behaviours such as rudeness, aggression, or refusal to comply with adults' instructions can teach children to behave in a manner that is socially inappropriate.

3.   Fictional reinforcement contingencies can exert powerful control over some children's behaviour. Beliefs that other children are dangerous can lead to avoidance of the playground, parties, and so on; many other irrational beliefs may be acquired through the remarks and teaching of other people or may be self-generated. These fictional reinforcement contingencies can be even more powerful than *real* external reinforcing conditions.

4.   Faulty self-reinforcement can occur when children hold unrealistically high standards for themselves and remain chronically dissatisfied with their achievements.

There are several examples of the successful use of contingent adult attention to increase peer interaction in pre-school children; differential adult reinforcement has served to reduce aggressive behaviour while increasing the kinds of competing behaviours which are thought to be socially desirable (see Herbert, 1986; 1987).

Cognitive approaches (problem-solving)

If psychological treatment can boost a client's perceived self-efficacy, then the client should be able to approach formerly dreaded situations with new confidence (Bandura, 1977). Heightened self-efficacy leads to more vigorous, persistent and probably more successful attempts to cope with the problem. Successful resolution of problems will in turn increase the child's perceived self-effectiveness even further. Bandura offers four major sources of self-efficacy expectations:

➤   performance accomplishments;

➤   modelling demonstrations;

➤   verbal persuasion; and

➤   emotional arousal.

There is evidence from research that young children who employ a wide range of alternative and competent strategies on problem-solving tasks tend to play more constructively, are better liked, and are less aggressive. Therefore the purpose of this component of the programme is to coach parents how they can teach their children appropriate problem-solving skills.

Questions parents ask about problem-solving

Shouldn't you tell children the correct solutions?

'I feel I need to tell my children how to solve the problem because they don't come up with the right answer on their own – in fact, some of their own solutions are really bad!'

Is there such a thing as too little guidance?

'Well, I just tell my children to work it out on their own. I think that's the only way children will learn to problem-solve. Don't you agree?'

Feelings don't have much to do with problem-solving, do they?

'I don't talk much about feelings with my children. What value is there in this?'

Many parents believe that telling their children how to solve a problem helps them learn to problem-solve. For example, two children may have trouble sharing a bicycle. The parent responds to the child who has grabbed the bicycle from the other child (who has refused to share the bike) by saying, 'You should either play together or take turns. Grabbing is not nice. You can't go around grabbing things. Would you like that if he did it to you?' The problem with this approach is that the parents are telling the children what to do before they have found out what the problem is from their viewpoint. It is possible, after all, that the parent has misdiagnosed the problem. For example, in this case it was not entirely the fault of the child who grabbed the bicycle because the other child had used the bike for a long time and had refused to share it even when asked nicely. As the child continued to refuse to share, the other child escalated to grabbing. Moreover, the parents' approach in this example does not help the children to think about their problem and how to solve it. Rather than being encouraged to *learn* how to think, they are *told* what to think, and the solution is imposed upon them.

The opposite problem occurs when parents think they are helping their children resolve conflict by telling them to work it out for themselves. This might work if the children already have good problem-solving skills; but for most young children this approach will not work. In a case where Pat and Amy are fighting over a book, non-intervention will probably result in continued arguing and Amy, the more aggressive child, getting the book. Therefore, Amy is reinforced for her inappropriate behaviour because she got what she wanted, and Pat is reinforced for giving in because the fighting ceased when she backed down.

Here are the main points to emphasize:

➤ **Help children define the problem.**

➤ **Talk about feelings.**

➤ **Involve children in brainstorming possible solutions.**

➤ **Be positive and imaginative.**

➤ **Model creative solutions.**

➤ **Encourage children to think through the possible consequences of different solutions.**

➤ **Remember that it is the process of learning how to think about the conflict that is critical, rather than getting 'correct' answers.**

Practitioners might suggest that the parents begin to teach their children these skills by role playing or acting them out with puppets or books. Recommend that these discussions occur at neutral times, not in the heat of battle. Once parents have taught children the steps and the language to talk about problems, they can then begin to help them learn how to use the skills in the midst of real conflict.

It is effective for parents to guide their children into thinking about what may have caused the problem in the first place, rather than to tell them the solution. Parents can invite their children to come up with possible solutions. If parents want to help them develop a habit of solving their own problems, children need to be asked to think for themselves. Parents can encourage their children to talk aloud as they think and then can praise their ideas and attempts at solutions. In this way the parents are reinforcing the development of a style of thinking that will help them to deal with all kinds of problems throughout their lives. After several possible solutions have been generated, parents can then help the child to shift their focus to the possible consequences of each solution. The final step in problem-solving is to help children evaluate their possible solutions. For children aged three to nine years, the second step – generating solutions – is the key skill to learn. While older children are more easily involved in anticipating consequences and evaluating them, youngsters need to be helped to generate possible solutions and to understand that some solutions are better than others. They should be urged to express their feelings about the situation, talk about ideas for solving the problem, and talk about what might happen if they carried out various solutions. The only time parents need to offer solutions is if their children need a few ideas to get them started.

The therapist should emphasize the importance of parental modelling as a way to teach children problem-solving skills. It is a rich learning experience for children to watch their parents working out resolutions to problems.

Conclusion

There seems little doubt that SST is a fruitful area for continuing use in clinical practice and further research. The vexed questions which arise in relation to SST are similar to those that are generated in any behavioural interventions with problematic children. The perennial question begging for answers, is the one about the *specific* ingredients which make for effective change in particular cases. Also unresolved is the technical problem of ensuring temporal and response generalization. The studies which I have quoted on SST are usually restricted to follow-up periods of a few weeks or months, and to a relatively narrow range of criterion social situations.

References

Bandura, A. (1977). *Social Learning Theory*. Englewood Cliff, NJ: Prentice-Hall.

Combs, M.L. and Slaby, D.A. (1977). Social skills training with children. In: B.B. Lahey and A.E. Kazdin (Eds) *Advances in Clinical Psychology, Vol. 1*. New York: Plenum.

Gresham, F.M. (1981). Validity of social skills for measuring for social competence in low-status children. *Developmental Psychology, 17*, 390–398.

Herbert, M. (1974). *Emotional Problems of Development in Children*. London: Academic Press.

Herbert, M. (1986). Social skills training with children. In: C.R. Hollin and P. Trower (Eds) *Handbook of Social Skills Training. Volume I: Applications across the life-span*. Oxford: Pergamon Press.

Herbert, M. (1987). *Behavioural Treatment of Children with Problems: A practice manual*. London: Academic Press.

Hops, H. (1983). Children's social competence and skill. *Behaviour Therapy, 14*, 3–18.

Kazdin, A.E. *et al.* (1981). Social skills performance among normal and psychiatric in-patient children as a function of assessment conditions. *Behaviour Research and Therapy, 19*, 145–152.

Ladd, G.W. (1984). Social skill training with children: Issues in research and practice. *Clinical Psychology Review, 4*, 317–337.

Webster-Stratton, C. and Herbert, M. (1994). *Troubled Families – Problem Children: A Collaborative Approach*. Chichester: Wiley.

Appendix I: Sunflower Charts

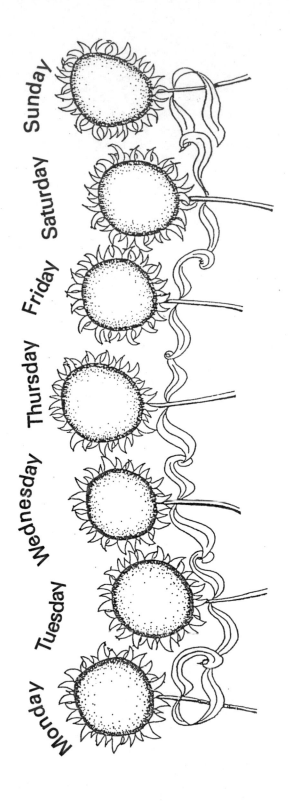

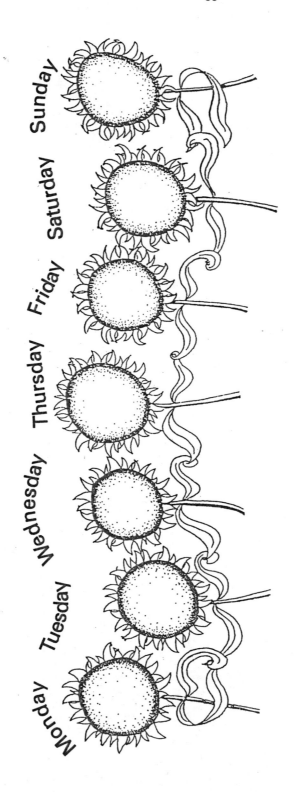

Monday Tuesday Wednesday Thursday Friday Saturday Sunday

Appendix II: People Charts

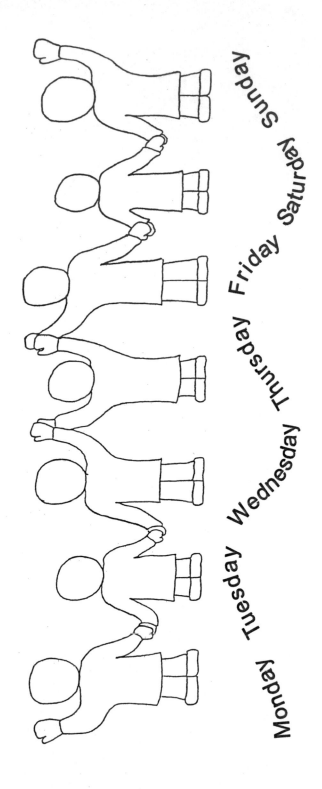

Monday Tuesday Wednesday Thursday Friday Saturday Sunday

Monday Tuesday Wednesday Thursday Friday Saturday Sunday

Appendix III: Football Charts

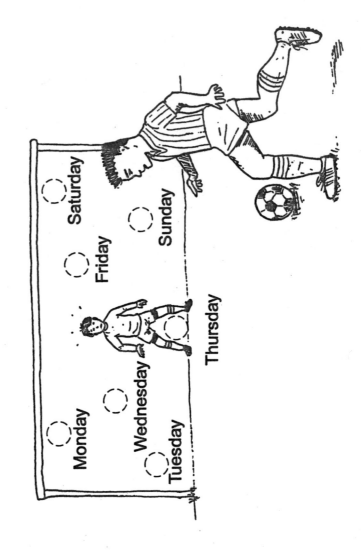

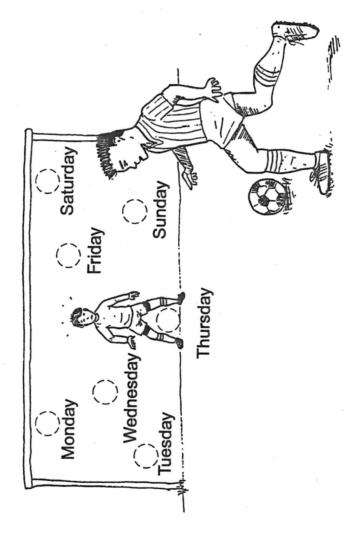

Note to the practitioner

Here follows some guidance in a form that can be related to, or given to, parents, preferably as a basis for a discussion with you — a preliminary to planning change-strategies. Three examples of reinforcement charts for children to colour in when treatment goals are reached are provided in the appendices to this guide. These were drawn for the Herbert–Wookey manual by Alex McCahearty.

Hints for Parents 1: Strengthening new behaviour patterns

Positive reinforcement

In order to improve or increase your child's performance of certain (say) sociable actions, arrange matters so that an immediate reward follows the correct performance of the desired behaviour. You might indicate your intentions by saying, for example, '*When* you have put your toys away, *then* you can go out'. The 'when – then' formula reminds you that you only reward after the desired action is carried out. When the child has learned a behaviour it is no longer necessary to give rewards regularly. Remember that words of praise and encouragement at such a stage can be very reinforcing. Colouring-in charts can be a useful incentive.

Developing new behaviour patterns

Encouragement

Secure your child's co-operation by guiding and helping him/her towards some desirable action or way of thought. Use a combination of suggestion, appreciation of his/her difficulties, praise for his/her efforts and pleasure at success.

In order to encourage your child to act in a way in which s/he has seldom or never before behaved, reward approximations to the correct action. You take your child through mini-steps towards a goal by rewarding any action that approximates the behaviour you want. You continue to reinforce the approximations to the behaviour you wish to elicit. No reinforcement is given to 'wrong' behaviours. Gradually you make your standards (criteria) of your child's approximations to the correct response more and more stringent until, in the end, s/he is only rewarded for the precise behavioural sequence that is required.

Modelling

In order to teach your child a new pattern of behaviour, give him/her the opportunity to observe a person who is significant to him/her performing the desired behaviour.

Skills training

Simulate real-life situations in which skills are to be developed. During rehearsal:

➤   demonstrate the skill;

➤   ask your child to practise the skill (use role play);

➤   provide a model if necessary;

➤   provide feedback as to the accuracy/inaccuracy of his/her performance. (If possible, it is advantageous for the youngster – and video equipment is most useful here – to evaluate the effectiveness of his/her own performance);

➤   give homework assignments, for example, real-life planned practice of skills. Not only does behaviour rehearsal provide for acquiring new skills but it also allows their practice at a controlled pace and in a safe environment, and in this way minimizes distress.

Cueing

In order to train your child to act at a specific time, arrange for her/ him to receive a cue for the correct performance just before the action is expected, rather than after s/he has performed incorrectly.

Discrimination

In order to teach your child to act in a particular manner under one set of circumstances but not another, train her/him to identify the cues that differentiate between the appropriate and inappropriate circumstances. Reward her/him only when his/her action is appropriate to the cue (for example, s/he is praised for crossing the pedestrian crossing when the signal is given).

The treatment agenda is not only about 'correctives' to socially unskilled or anti-social behaviour. You need principles and practical techniques for encouraging and maintaining not only socially skilled actions, but also other prosocial behaviours. In relation to this point it is important to check what you are asking of your child, and on what has or has not been taught them. Children can hardly be blamed for not doing what they don't know, are not capable of.

The following questions are pertinent:

➤ Are the expectations of the child reasonable?

➤ Does s/he know *what* to do?

➤ Does s/he know *how* to do it?

➤ Does s/he know *when* to do it?

Of course, children may have been taught, and know, the socially appropriate behaviour or skill and when to produce it but still not perform it. So there are four more questions:

➤ How can I get him/her to do what I want him/her to do?

➤ Now that s/he does it, how can I encourage him/her to continue doing it?

➤ How can I get him/her to stop doing what I don't want him/her to do?

➤ Now that s/he has stopped doing it, how can I encourage him/her to continue to desist from doing it?

Hints for Parents 2: Social skills and friendship

Youngsters who cannot get on with other children, who are lacking in social skills, who are clumsy or shy, often lead miserable and lonely lives. They may lack the vital skills of social sensitivity, being able to make small talk, and of forming accurate impressions of other people – the foundations upon which personal liking, leading to the attraction of acquaintances, and thereby to friendship, is built. Those children who are the most popular or influential members of groups, and the most effective leaders, tend to have these attributes in abundance. Of course, there are children who possess the requisite social skills but have little opportunity to practise them and thus gain confidence.

The emphasis in friendships is on mutual satisfaction of needs. There must always be some give-and-take; friendships which are too one-sided, selfish or exploitive, are not likely to last. To continue with the economic analogy, when costs soar and the balance-sheet is in fundamental imbalance, showing persistent losses, the friendship is likely to be in danger.

Choosing friends

The process by which people are initially attracted to each other and finally become friends, can be represented symbolically by a 'funnel' with a series of filters in it. Each person has such a figurative 'funnel', with filters designed to fit his/her particular criteria for a friend. At the opening of the funnel is the first criterion, *proximity,* which determines the eligibles. Before any kind of attraction can be established there must be opportunity for the children to come into contact. Ordinarily, friendships evolve out of some direct face-to-face contact. Children who live close to one another are more likely to become friends than those who live some distance apart, and children who interact frequently are more likely to become friends than those who interact rarely. Youngsters who live in isolated areas, or whose parents artificially isolate them from other children, may have difficulty in making friends. The pool of eligibles is too small for making contacts, choices or for learning to interact socially with peers.

Further filters will work to narrow the field gradually. In general, the filters select 'similar individual characteristics', 'common interests or values', and 'similar personality'. Someone who successfully passes through these filters becomes a friend. The second filter works on the basis that *like attracts like*. There is little or no evidence that opposites attract in children's friendships. Pairs of friends, in fact, tend to resemble each other in several respects: social maturity, age, weight, height and general intelligence. Friendly, energetic, capable, responsive and daring youngsters are attracted to each other, possibly because they understand one another and can fulfil their mutual needs. Thus, the second filter suggests that birds of a feather do flock together.

Friendship choices are influenced to a significant extent by similarities in social background, religious affiliations and ethnic group membership. The most significant influence on the formation of friendships is the *belief* that another is similar to oneself; this is more important than whether or not s/he is *actually* similar. Children also tend to choose as friends those with characteristics considered desirable in terms of the values of their group.

Helping your child

If you are worried about your child's inability to make or keep friends, carry out a small exercise in 'accountancy', based on discreet observations of your youngster's behaviour with other children; the trick is to look at things from the *other* child's point of view. Is your child being insensitive, too demanding, or disloyal? Is his/her company rewarding enough?

Practical hints

Teach him/her

Teach your child to see the other's point of view (not necessarily at the expense of his/her own). Role-taking – the mental placing of oneself in the other person's position – is central to all forms of human communication. There is evidence that children engage in rudimentary forms of role-taking very early in life. Nevertheless, when children are confronted with perspectives that are different from their own, they often *assume* similarity where there is none. This leads to misunderstanding – mutual and, at times, painful.

Praise him/her

Praise your child for initiating social behaviour.

Model for him/her

Model (set an example of) *social* behaviour to a child; physically demonstrate the various ways of interacting socially with others. Demonstrate how s/he might make positive comments about another child: also show him/her how to play constructively.

Prompt him/her

Ask your child to demonstrate something to another (for example, how to work the fizzy drinks machine); direct him/her to help, or seek help, of another.

Coach him/her

Coach your child in social behaviour – encourage him/her in social activity and describe or explain ways of interacting socially , for example, when s/he is with children you have invited home. Here are some suggestions:

➤ Encourage the child to adopt a sociable perspective (for example, 'Let's talk about some ways to have fun with other children when you play games'; 'One way to make a game fun for everyone is to take turns ... when you take turns in a game other children will have fun too and will want to play with you again').

➤ Clarify what 'taking turns' means (for example, 'During a game, taking turns means giving everyone a chance to play').

➤ Encourage your child to identify some good and bad examples (for example, 'Yes, waiting until others have finished before you begin would be taking turns'; 'Always trying to have first go or stopping others from having a try would not be taking turns').

➤ Get your child to rehearse verbally some examples of sociable actions and then to recall them.

➤ Give your child 'feedback' about the way s/he has learned (and later, hopefully, performs) the social skill.

In this way you teach your child to translate social ideas and values into social actions.